Explore the Outdoors

Snowmobiling

Have Fun, Be Smart

By Michael A. Sommers

Published in 2000 by The Rosen Publishing Group, Inc.
29 East 21st Street, New York, NY 10010

First Edition

Sommers, Michael A., 1966–
   Snowmobiling : have fun, be smart / by Michael Sommers.
     p. cm. — (Explore the outdoors)
  Includes bibliographical references and index.
  ISBN 0-8239-3171-4
   1. Snowmobiling. 2. Snowmobiling—Safety measures. I. Title. II. Series.
GV856.5 .S64 2000
796.94—dc21   99-054847
                                          CIP
                                          AC

Manufactured in the United States of America

Contents

Introduction

When Sam moved with his family from Arizona to Vermont, he started to hate Thanksgiving. Not Thanksgiving itself—he loved feasting on turkey, stuffing, and cranberry sauce. He hated what came after Thanksgiving: winter.

Sam considered himself a summer kind of guy. He loved playing baseball and tennis, going hiking in the desert, even just sitting outside in the sun and reading a book. The thing about Arizona was that there summer lasted basically all year long. In Vermont, it wasn't unusual for snow to start falling as early as November and to last up until April. Sam hated the cold. It seemed that he spent most of his weekends cooped up in the house—watching television, playing video games, and feeling cranky. Meanwhile, most of his buddies were busy doing things like skiing and playing hockey. Sam had tried playing hockey with some of the guys, but they had been shooting the puck around for years, and his skills were not as advanced as theirs. Sam decided that he wasn't that into hockey anyway.

Then one Saturday morning in January, when Sam had a particularly bad case of the winter blues, his dad walked into the darkened den where Sam was staring at the television. His dad

Winter is the time to get out the snowmobile.

tossed a down jacket, a pair of thermal gloves, and a woolen cap on Sam's lap and slapped him on the back. "Come on, kid," he grinned. "Time to get off your butt, get bundled up, and enjoy the winter wonderland outside."

Sam sighed and gave his dad what he hoped was an irritated glare. His dad just kept on grinning. He motioned for Sam to get dressed and follow him outside. After the gloomy darkness of the TV room, Sam felt blinded by the brightness of the sun sparkling on fresh white snow. He inhaled deeply. The air was pure and clean.

Together they got into the car and drove a few miles out of the small town where Sam's family was living. The passing hills and forests, all covered in a blanket of white, seemed very inviting. Then Sam's dad pulled up in front of a big wooden building. In an adjacent lot, Sam could see about twenty shiny metallic snowmobiles. They looked like high-tech sleds on skis.

"What's up, Dad?" asked Sam.

"This is our local snowmobile club, son," explained Sam's dad as he got out of the car. "I signed both of us up for some lessons. We're going to learn how to operate snowmobiles and how to drive them safely. With a little patience, we'll even get to try a couple out before the day is over."

"Snowmobiling, huh?" Sam pondered, shooting his dad a questioning look.

"Yeah, snowmobiling. As in you and me, all wrapped up and speeding through the snowy wilderness. Trees flying by, deer and beaver, the great outdoors—you're going to love this, son."

"I sure hope so," said Sam a little doubtfully, as he followed his dad up the stairs and into the snowmobiling club.

1 What Is Snowmobiling All About?

Snowmobiles are not confined to trails or fixed routes.

Snowmobiling is definitely an activity that makes winter worthwhile. Each year in Canada and the United States, millions of men, women, and kids of all ages decide that hibernation is for the birds (and the bears) and take to the 230,000 miles of public and private trails that weave through states and provinces.

One of the best things about snowmobiling is that it has so many different aspects. Although it is an individual sport—just you and your "sled" zooming through the snow—at the same time, it is a great way to spend some time in the outdoors with friends or family. Snowmobiling combines the thrill and skill of maneuvering a fast and powerful machine with an active workout that is healthy for both your mind and your body. This is why at the end of a hard day on the trail, you feel so relaxed—both mentally and physically.

Over the last few years, snowmobiling has grown increasingly popular in North America, particularly with families. These days there are more than two million snowmobiles registered in both Canada and the United States and over 3,000 snowmobiling clubs in both countries. In addition, there are twelve provincial and territorial snowmobile associations in Canada and twenty-seven state associations in the United States. There is a snowmobiling professional race circuit. There are snowmobile museums and snowmobile collectors. There is even an International Snowmobiling Hall of Fame (in Bovey, Minnesota). Snowmobiling magazines, e-zines, and Web sites are all over the place. And snowmobile fashion—from boots and socks to helmets and goggles—is hotter, not to mention warmer, than ever before.

The North American Snowmobile Trail System

The first explorers to trudge across North America's wilderness carved a whole series of trails through the brush. For years and even centuries afterward, future travelers were able to use these paths, knowing that they were safe and

A "groomed" snowmobile trail

well kept. This North American tradition of carving and maintaining trails is very much alive among today's snowmobiling communities.

Across North America's snow country, snowmobilers meet and form clubs that are about more than just having a good time sledding. These snowmobile clubs work together with state and provincial associations to create and monitor snowmobiling laws. They publish newsletters, organize a host of winter activities, and sponsor snowmobile trips and outings. Many club members are certified safety training instructors who can help you get started by teaching you everything you need to know about snowmobiling.

Not only do these instructors offer courses to the public on snowmobile safety and machine maintenance, but they also organize special snowmobile search-and-rescue units. Such units aid everyone from police and sheriff's departments to wildlife conservation officers. Perhaps most important, however, these clubs and their members design, maintain, and pay for a complex system of marked trails. Such well-kept trails ensure that snowmobilers have fun and ride safely throughout the North American snowbelt.

All in the Family

More than 94.5 percent of those who take part in snowmobiling consider it to be a family sport.

These trails, which run on private and public land, are the lifeblood of snowmobiling. Close to 80 percent of North America's three million snowmobilers ride on such trails, which are marked—or "groomed." Some of them have been around for as many as thirty years. Of all the snowmobiling states and provinces, Wisconsin has the most—25,000 miles worth, to be precise. However, the provinces of Ontario and Quebec and the state of Minnesota are quickly catching up.

The way this works is that a group of volunteers belonging to a local snowmobiling club see a need for a trail. They seek permission from government authorities (if the trail is to run over public land, such as a national park) or from a private landowner (if the trail is to wind through a privately owned field or patch of woods) before beginning to organize and build a trail. This is usually done in cooperation with provincial, state, and local governments, as is the continued upkeep of the trail. Although each state or province has its own snowmobiling system and its own way of paying for it, in the end, most of this money comes from permit and registration

More Than Just Fun and Games

Whereas 80 percent of snowmobilers zoom around for pleasure, 20 percent use their sleds for work. In particularly chilly parts of Canada and the United States, snowmobiles are used by everybody from ranchers, environmentalists, and cross-country ski race officials to police officers, phone company employees, and ice fishers.

fees paid by snowmobilers themselves.

The exciting thing about these trails is that instead of just being scattered individually throughout the countryside, many are actually connected to each other. In the United States, Midwest and East Coast states have many "integrated" trails that hook up with one another. This means that you can sled for days without having to jump off your snowmobile. In Canada, the situation is even cooler. In 1998, the Trans Canada Snowmobile Trail—a 6,200-mile snowmobiling corridor connecting the Pacific to the Atlantic coast (with extensions to the northern territories)—was finally completed. To inaugurate it, the Canadian Council of Snowmobile Organizations produced Power Streak Rendez-Vous '98, in which sixteen gutsy "sled heads" spent forty-three days zooming from Newfoundland to British Columbia. With this constantly expanding network of trails, you can now sled not only from province to province and state to state but from country to country as well.

In snowmobile country, you can find trail maps as

The Best of the Best Trails
1. Upper Peninsula, Michigan
2. Northwoods, Wisconsin
3. West Yellowstone, Montana
4. North Shore, Minnesota

Source: Snow Goer *magazine's annual SnowTime Awards*

easily as road maps. This is because in many regions, snowmobiles are used more than other types of vehicles. Such is the case in the new Canadian territory of Nunavut, for example, where snowmobiles largely outnumber cars.

Often trails don't just lead over the snow and through the woods. They link towns and resorts, restaurants and gas stations, parks and parking lots. Trail maps point out not only snowmobiling trails, shelters, and rest areas but also hospitals, towns, and other useful landmarks. They also provide a list of the snowmobiling groups that created and now maintain the trails, along with their contact numbers. These are good to have for safety reasons—or if you're in the mood to hook up with some fellow "powder hounds."

Aside from helping you plan your trip, trail maps are important because they allow you to leave a "snow plan" with your friends and family. A snow plan lists your planned route and destination. It also provides a description of your sled. This way, if you don't arrive at your final destination on time, your pals and relatives know where to look for you. (If you do arrive at your final destination on time, make sure to let these folks know so that nobody goes searching for you needlessly.)

2 History of Snowmobiling

It has been a long and snowy trail since the first snowmobiles came into being, back in the early 1920s. The snowmobile was created when garage inventors stuck skis onto the fronts of old cars, doubled the rear wheels, and hit the slopes.

An early snowmobile

The first snowmobiles were built for work, not for fun. A few of them were large enough to carry ten or twelve people. They were used by doctors and veterinarians as ambulances and taxis that could transport people and animals over deep snow to safety. Hunters and foresters were other buyers of early snowmobiles.

It wasn't until decades later, however, that the makers of snowmobiles caught on to the fact that whipping through the snow was just plain fun. These manufacturers began to make and sell a new, more sophisticated type of snowmobile geared toward people who wanted to ride for recreation.

The Birth of the Motor Toboggan

Carl Eliason was only twenty-four years old when he first drove his hand-built Motor Toboggan through the woods near Sayner, Wisconsin. This grandfather of all snowmobiles was built by Carl in a garage behind his general store. It took him two years of working in his spare time to perfect the machine.

The small snowmobile he patented in 1924 was basically a long wooden sled powered by a 2.5-horsepower outboard motor engine. The machine also featured a dual-chain track system made out of bicycle parts (Carl took a long train trip to Milwaukee just to purchase them), two downhill skis that were steered by ropes, and part of a Ford Model T radiator, used for cooling the motor when it overheated.

Over the next fifteen years, Carl built and sold forty snowmobiles out of Sayner. Almost every one was different. As snowmobiles grew larger—seating three to four people instead of just two—they were outfitted with motorcycle engines. At this point, they were purchased mostly by hunters and utility workers.

During World War II, the United States Army purchased 150 completely white Eliason Motor Toboggans to use in the defense of Alaska. A group of Russians also came to test-drive Carl's snowmobiles. They borrowed a machine gun from the local library, set it on the front of the sled, and test-drove it up and down Pigeon River, shooting imaginary bullets at the riverbank.

After the war boom, however, production tapered off. Snowmobiles were now being purchased primarily by trappers and state wildlife conservationists. In the 1950s, production moved to Canada. It was here that the last Eliason snowmobile was built—the scarlet K-12 sled with its revolutionary rear engine. By then, though, the bright yellow Ski-Doos were taking the snowmobiling world by storm. In 1964, production of Eliason snowmobiles came to a halt.

Today, the Vilas County Historical Society Museum in Sayner, Wisconsin, houses Carl's original hand-built snowmobile as well as one of each Eliason model ever produced. The K-12 —in addition to Carl's other snowmobiles—has become a collector's item.

It was in the 1960s that lightweight one- and two-person recreational snowmobiles came into being. The super-modern Ski-Doo—invented by snowmobiling pioneer Joseph-Armand Bombardier—revolutionized the machine with a design that still sets the standard for today's snowmobiles. Also, the development of a gas engine allowed for much smaller snowmobiles to be built.

Not surprisingly, these new machines were a big hit. But just as in nature, only the fittest were able to survive ever-changing tastes and demands. For a while, close to 100 companies were busy building and selling snowmobiles. Today, only four big guns remain—Polaris, Arctic Cat (Arctco), Bombardier, and Yamaha. The sleds they are coming out with now make the machines of the 1960s and '70s look like antiques.

The Big Chill

In February 1968, American Ralph Plaisted and his posse of sledders set out from Montreal, Quebec, upon their Ski-Doo Olympiques. For the next forty-three days, they roughed it through -60°F temperatures and violent snowstorms, riding over 20-foot-high ice ridges and narrow crevices that suddenly filled with crashing ocean waves. Incredibly, 826 miles later they finally made it. They got off their sleds and set foot on the North Pole!

Modern suspension systems make for safer, more stable rides.

The biggest changes in snowmobiling came in the early 1990s. Better suspension systems make for better rides. Improved shock absorbers now take the bumps that used to be reserved for your body. Bigger machines with larger tracks offer the increased stability and comfort of a big, cushy-seated car. Clean lines and state-of-the-art technology, coupled with increased comfort and safety, have been responsible for the surge in snowmobile mania. Whatever changes the future may bring, it is certain that the snow-mobile will be around for a long time to come.

The World's Smallest Snowmobile

Its name was the Little Skipper. It weighed less than 100 pounds and it came in three colors— red, yellow, and gold. It was the first-ever snow-mobile made for an as yet unexplored market— kids between the ages of seven and twelve.

Between 1970 and 1973, close to 1,000 Little Skippers were made. They were so small and light that even their young riders could lift them.

Initial response to the midget machines was overwhelming. But lack of snow and lack of dough caused production to falter.

Then along came kiddie competition—Arctic Cat's Kitty Cat. Things were looking ugly until the two rivals took to the track. The Little Skipper— whose top speed was 30 mph—soon took care of the Kitty Cat, which at 10 mph was quite literally left in the dust.

Although the Little Skipper itself bit the dust in 1973, today it is a serious collector's item and an important part of snowmobiling history.

3 The Right Stuff

No matter what sport you're into, it is essential that you have the right stuff. You want to be as secure and protected as possible. You also want to have equipment that performs well, allowing you to experience the maximum amount of pleasure.

With snowmobiling, buying and maintaining

the proper equipment is especially important. Remember that this is a high-speed sport that is practiced in the chilly outdoors. These are risks that can be dangerous if you don't have the right equipment and don't take the proper safety precautions. This is why, first and foremost, it is essential to have a good sled that is in tip-top shape. You don't want a machine that hasn't been safety approved or one that will break down in the middle of the freezing countryside.

Sled Security

Snowmobiles these days are safer, more comfortable, and perform better than ever before. They are also quieter. New adjustable brake handles are perfect for young riders with smaller hands and shorter fingers. Brand-new hydraulic disc brakes will keep you safe and let you stop in no time at all.

Winter riding has never been so warm either. Heated handgrips and thumbgrips keep your fingers from freezing off, windshields are tall enough so that arctic winds pass right over you, and hoods are designed to reduce streams of icy air.

Snowmobile machine safety standards programs are sponsored throughout Canada and the United States by the Snowmobile Safety and Certification Committee (SSCC), an association that promotes safe snowmobiling. Under the SSCC program, machines are tested by an independent company that checks all the important parts of the sled—from electrical, lighting, and brake systems to reflectors, shields, and guards. This is to make absolutely sure that all parts are safe. A snowmobile that has been approved by the SSCC will have a black-and-white label located on its right rear tunnel. Make sure that you and

opposite: Protection from wind and cold is essential.

The SSCC safety label

your parents look for this label whenever riding, renting, or buying a snowmobile.

Brain Buckets

Aside from your machine, probably the most important piece of equipment you will buy will be your helmet. Whether you call it a "brain bucket," a "lid," or a "foam dome," a helmet is there to protect your head from getting injured. In the case of snowmobiling, helmets serve another purpose—to keep your head warm. Although some snowmobilers think that they are too cool for helmets—they like the sensation of their hair flowing in the arctic breeze—riding helmetless is both dumb and dangerous.

Finding the right helmet often comes down to two things: your personal preference and the shape of your head. There are a whole bunch of colors, styles, and graphics to choose from, but what really counts is how well a foam dome fits and protects you.

Snowmobiling helmets are made out of two materials: fiberglass and polycarbonate. Fiberglass helmets, which tend to be more expensive because they take longer to make, are made of thin layers of fiberglass. Polycarbonate helmets—

A "brain bucket"

generally cheaper, since they are easier to make—are made by squirting liquid plastic (polycarbonate) into a helmet form. Both helmets protect in different ways. During a crash, a fiberglass helmet will break into pieces, whereas a polycarbonate one will stay intact.

Inside your "lid" is a plastic foam interior that will absorb the shock in a crash. Also on the inside are pads and other comfort features. It is essential that before buying a helmet, you try it on and make sure that it fits well. This means that it should be snug but shouldn't pinch. When your head moves, the helmet should move as well. With kids especially, a helmet should never be too big.

Keep in mind, however, that you will probably be wearing some kind of headgear inside your helmet. Finally, any helmet you buy should have a DOT rating—meaning that it has passed safety tests administered by the U.S. Department of Transportation (DOT).

Helmets can cost any-where between $50 and $400. Although it's important to invest in a good-quality brain bucket that you know is safe, there are ways of bringing down the price. Solid-color helmets, for example, are cheaper than ones with styling graphics that sport the trendy brand names of the four big manufacturers.

Don't let the sharp turns throw you!

Basic Emergency Equipment

Always be prepared for an emergency. A good question to ask is, "Can I get back safely with the equipment I'm taking?" Here are some items to bring along:

First-aid kit
Tool kit (with spare parts)
Pocketknife
50 feet of nylon rope
Compass
Waterproof matches
Energy bars or other high-protein foods
Extra key (in case the original gets lost in
     the snow)
Snowshoes
Flashlight
Flares
Tube tent
Sunblock

The Proper Duds

Good news for sled heads—while snowmobiles have gotten more stylish, comfortable, and high-tech over time, so too have snowmobiling duds. These days, new materials keep snowmobilers warmer than ever before. There are many lines of clothing designed specifically for the chilly rigors of sledding. Far from being lumpy, clumpy, and making you look (and feel) like the abominable snowman, today's snowmobiling threads are lightweight and trendy, as well as windproof.

Aside from jackets and boots, neck coverings, gloves, face shields, and even helmets are specially designed to look cool but act warm. Most of these threads boast a series of layers that keep you extra toasty. An outer layer of fabric seals out

Today's powerful machines make for an exhilarating ride.

the wind and cold air, middle layers of insulating fabric separate the winter chill from your natural body warmth, and warm inner layers keep you dry and comfortable.

Wearing multiple layers of clothing is a very good idea. This way you can add or remove a layer or two depending on whether the weather gets colder or warmer. Especially important are warm gloves or mitts, boots, and a helmet. Shades or goggles with a good sun filter are also useful, and along with your helmet and face shield, they will also protect you from flying twigs, stones, or chips of ice. Also, don't forget a visor—it will protect you from the wind and allow you to see clearly.

A lot of this snowmobile clothing is designed by snowmobile makers themselves. In fact, it has become really hip to sport brand names. Some riders like to match their machines in terms of colors, logos, and graphics. Remember, though, that looking cool is never as important as staying warm and safe.

4 Safety First

In previous chapters, you read about many aspects of snow-mobiling that have improved over the years to help make the sport much safer. There are the trails, which are carefully groomed and maintained. There are the machines and equipment, which are much more precise and come with loads of safety features. Of course, riding with the best equipment upon the best trails is not enough. To be safe and have fun on a snowmobile means taking proper precautions. You must learn rules and regulations and be aware of both your environment and other riders.

Basic safety means knowing how to ride properly and how your machine works. All provinces and states offer snowmobile operator safety-training programs. In most places, they are obligatory for young drivers under the age of sixteen. In the state of Colorado, for example, by law anyone between the ages of ten and sixteen who wants to ride a snowmobile on public land must be safety certified or supervised by an adult who has been. In order for riders to become safety certified, Colorado state parks, the Colorado Snowmobile Association, and all local snowmobile clubs offer free safety-training courses that combine six hours of classroom instruction with an opportunity to actually try out a snowmobile. (You don't have to own one to take the class.) Successful completion of such a course will give you a certificate in snowmobile safety.

At the same time, the International Snowmobile Manufacturers Association—a group created by the four major snowmobile manufacturers themselves—promotes safe snowmobiling through the "Safe Riders! You Make Snowmobiling Safe" campaign. They distribute free information throughout Canada and the United States, discussing various rules, regulations, and safety tips.

Equally important is getting to know your machine by reading the manual that comes with it. Boring? Perhaps. Essential reading? Without a doubt. Finally, don't forget that at the beginning of each winter season—just like you—your snowmobile should have a mechanical checkup to make sure that everything is in perfect condition.

Learn to read the snow to avoid cravasses.

A Sled Head's Checklist

Get Ready...
* Know the terrain you are going to ride in advance—and make sure that you're permitted to ride on it.
* Check the weather forecast—especially ice and snow conditions.
* Make sure that your machine is in top shape and is properly registered in the area in which you are riding.

Get Set...
* File a "snow plan" with the trail you plan to ride, your destination, and a description of your machine.
* Fill up your tank.
* Make sure that you are carrying a first-aid kit, a tool kit, extra clothes, and basics such as a map and a pocketknife.

Go!
* Keep your feet on the sled when going downhill or riding on wooded trails.
* Pump your brake when going downhill to avoid locking the brakes.
* Lean into turns with your upper body. This will help you steer your sled more smoothly.

Signs

Learning all about your machine and how to operate it is only part of snowmobiling safety. Another important part is knowing the rules of the road—or, in the case of snowmobiling, of the trail.

Snowmobiling rules and laws can change depending on what state, province, or region you're in. Make sure that you know ahead of time what the local deal is by checking out

Snowmobile trail sign

maps, Web sites, or information from local clubs. In general, be especially careful when the trail cuts across private land. Stay off ski trails and always yield the right of way to those passing or traveling uphill. Above all, remember that whenever the trail meets a road or highway, you should come to a full stop and make sure that no traffic is approaching from any direction. You should cross the road at a right angle to traffic.

Zooming around on your sled, you will come upon certain signs that give you information about the trail ahead. It is important to be familiar with some of the most common ones.

Hand Signals

When you're traveling in a group of snowmobilers, it's essential that you know how to communicate with other riders. Using hand signals is how riders exchange messages with one another on a trail. You must know not only how to read the

* Stop—Silver letters on a red background. Warns you to stop in front of an upcoming road crossing.

* Stop Ahead—Black letters on a yellow background. Warns you that there is a stop sign coming up ahead and to slow down in preparation.

* Danger—Black letters on a yellow background. Warns of a dangerous area on the trail.

* Trail Intersection—Black vertical stripe crossed by a black diagonal stripe, on a yellow background. Warns you of an upcoming intersection in the trail.

* Snowmobiling Permitted—White snowmobile on a brown background. Indicates trails and areas where snowmobiling is permitted.

* Snowmobiling Not Permitted—White snowmobile with a red diagonal stripe across it, on a brown background. Indicates areas where snowmobiling is not permitted.

* Continuing Trail—Orange with reflective border. Indicates that the trail still continues.

* Change Directions—Black arrow against an orange background. Indicates that the trail ahead will turn in the direction of the arrow.

signals the rider in front of you is giving, but how to pass a message on to the rider behind you. Don't give sloppy signs, and make sure that the person behind you can see your signals. The following approved signals should be used all the time:

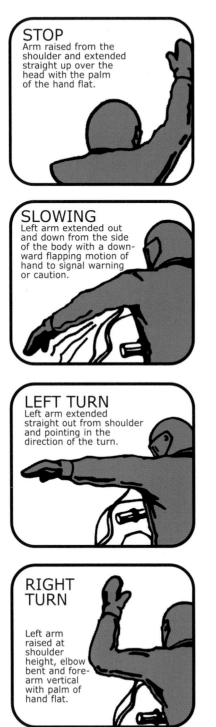

STOP
Arm raised from the shoulder and extended straight up over the head with the palm of the hand flat.

SLOWING
Left arm extended out and down from the side of the body with a downward flapping motion of hand to signal warning or caution.

LEFT TURN
Left arm extended straight out from shoulder and pointing in the direction of the turn.

RIGHT TURN
Left arm raised at shoulder height, elbow bent and forearm vertical with palm of hand flat.

* **Stop**—Raise your right hand straight up in the air, with your palm flat.

* **Slowing Down**— Raise your left arm straight out and wave your left hand downward.

* **Left Turn**—Point your left hand and arm straight out.

* **Right Turn**— Stretch out your left arm, bend it at the elbow, and point your left hand straight up.

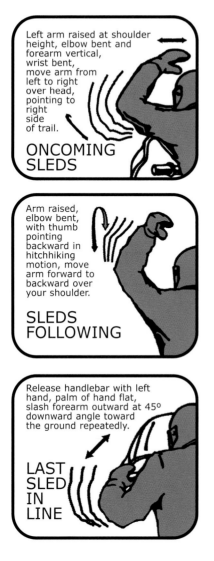

Left arm raised at shoulder height, elbow bent and forearm vertical, wrist bent, move arm from left to right over head, pointing to right side of trail.

ONCOMING SLEDS

Arm raised, elbow bent, with thumb pointing backward in hitchhiking motion, move arm forward to backward over your shoulder.

SLEDS FOLLOWING

Release handlebar with left hand, palm of hand flat, slash forearm outward at 45° downward angle toward the ground repeatedly.

LAST SLED IN LINE

* Oncoming Snowmobile—Move over to the right-hand side of the trail. Raise your left arm straight out. Wave your hand from left to right, signaling for the rider behind to move as far right as possible.

* Sleds Following—Raise your left arm and with your elbow bent, raise your thumb hitchhike style and move it from front to back over your shoulder. (This indicates to oncoming snowmobilers that there are other riders behind you.)

* Last Sled in Line—Push your left arm straight out repeatedly, waving your flat palm up and down at a 45-degree angle. (This indicates to oncoming snowmobilers that there are no other riders behind you.)

These signs, created by the Canadian Council of Snowmobiling Organizations (CCSO), have been approved by the American Council of Snowmobile Associations and the International Snowmobile Council. Information about them can be found through any snowmobiling club and on a variety of Web sites listed at the back of this book.

Don't Sled Sloshed

Drinking and snowmobiling are like peanut butter and salami—they simply don't go together.

Forget all that St. Bernard hogwash about how alcohol warms up a chilled person. What it actually does is open up your blood vessels. This takes away the feeling of cold but does nothing to increase your body heat. Instead, it increases the risks of hypothermia—a life-threatening condition in which your body temperature plunges.

Alcohol also makes you tired and slows your reflexes. It can have catastrophic consequences not only for you but for anyone unlucky enough to be riding behind you, in front of you, or across your path. Furthermore, driving a snowmobile while under the influence of alcohol is against the law.

Respecting the Environment

One of the best things about snowmobiling is riding over hills, through forests, and alongside lakes and experiencing some of the most spectacular natural landscapes that North America has to offer. You might ride on public trails that wind through state or national parks. More frequently, you'll probably find yourself on private trails, created with the permission of an individual property owner.

No matter

Trails are less safe in unfamiliar terrain.

what trail you take, it is essential—not only for other snowmobilers but for all nature lovers—that you respect the region through which you're riding, as well as the wildlife that lives there. This means don't run over trees and bushes and don't snowmobile in areas where the snow isn't deep enough to protect the vegetation. It means to leave a trail the way you left it—without breaking branches or leaving litter.

Of course, pollution doesn't apply just to garbage; it applies to noise as well. Some snowmobilers get a real charge out of cranking their motor. They exchange the factory-installed muffler for one that makes more *vrooom*. Or they add a straight pipe like the ones racers use in competitions. This only scares away animals and irritates other recreationists, not to mention the people over whose private property you might be riding. It also decreases your snowmobile's performance.

Respecting nature means not only appreciating it but being aware of its possible dangers. Lakes and rivers are definitely things you should be cautious about. The smartest idea is never to cross them. Not only do you risk plunging through the ice and into freezing cold water, but on ice you also have much less traction for starting, stopping, and changing direction. Furthermore, numerous snowmobiling accidents take place on lakes. This is because many people mistakenly think that lakes are completely flat, without any strange lumps or bumps to crash into.

If you do snowmobile on ice, be totally sure that it is truly frozen. You might be surprised to know that drowning is a leading cause of snowmobile deaths. For extra safety, buy a snowmobile suit that floats. In the unlucky event that you do go through the ice, your snowmobile suit and helmet will probably keep you afloat for a few minutes. Stay calm and try to slide back onto the ice by kicking your feet and using a sharp object to dig into the ice for support. If the ice continues to break, don't panic. Keep moving toward the shore,

Thin ice on lake surfaces can be dangerous.

remembering never to remove your gloves or mittens. Once you make it back on the ice, roll away from the hole. Don't stand up until you're sure that the ground is stable. To avoid hypothermia, have your body rubbed vigorously to get your circulation going. Then change immediately into dry, warm clothes. Drink plenty of warm liquids, but absolutely nothing containing alcohol.

Like lakes and rivers, mountains too can prove dangerous to snowmobilers. Mountain snowmobiling can be a spectacular thrill, yet you should never attack the Rockies or the Cascades before having received special mountain-riding training. Mountain riding involves certain risks—specifically, avalanches. Often, avalanche areas are marked or closed off altogether. If you're sledding in the mountains, you should always carry avalanche beacons, shovels, and a probe pole (to help find people buried in snow), as well as a portable radio in case you need to call for help.

Night Riding

Night riding is great for many reasons. It is usually the best—and only—time that sledders can get together during the week. By the time kids are home from school, parents are home from work, and dinner has been chomped down, it is dark out. Heading out into a quiet winter landscape, snow glittering against a starry night, can be a magical experience.

However, riding in the dark means taking extra precautions. At night, there is a great danger of crashing into things that are easily visible by day.

Also, estimating distances and the direction in which you are traveling can prove tricky. Here are some tips for after-hours sledding:

1. Make sure that your lights are working well and that your taillights are free of snow.

2. Don't overdrive your machine's headlights. Snowmobile headlights work well only at reduced speeds.

3. Don't sled on unknown trails or terrain.

4. Carry a flashlight or flare for emergency signaling.

5. Because your visibility is lower, don't drive as fast as you would during the day.

6. Be extra careful if freezing rain starts to fall—among other things, your goggles may freeze over.

5 The World of Snowmobiling

Snowmobiling used to be just for hunters, Inuits, and hearty, outdoorsy types. Not anymore. Today more than 40 percent of people riding North America's marked trails are women and children.

Snowmobiling has entered the mainstream, and there really is a world of snowmobiling. As a means of transportation, snowmobiles can go places that no other motorized vehicle can. As a business, snowmobiling generates more than $9 billion in North America each year. As a recreational pastime, snowmobiling is taking off as never before. And as an increasingly recognized sport, competitive snowmobiling is suddenly exploding.

Snowcross Racing

Competitive snowmobile racing across a challenging chunk of icy terrain—known as snowcross racing—is the winter rage in the snowy states and provinces of North America. The most important races are heavily attended by fans and are increasingly broadcast by television networks such as ESPN.

This popularity led to snowcross racing being the first motorized sport to be included in ESPN's Winter X Games—a made-for-television extreme sports Olympics. The 1998 coverage allowed other young sports fans to discover what snow-cross racing fans already knew—that a nonstop, twenty- to thirty-vehicle snowcross race is exciting to watch and looks especially good on television, where you can get a great view of the speed, the jumps, and the vibrant colors.

For those not yet ready for the Sport, Semipro, or Pro levels but inter-

Competitive racing is becoming popular.

ested in getting involved in competitive sledding, both Canada and the United States have snowcross racing associations that organize races for snowmobilers of all levels and ages. First-year racers who are just starting can compete against one another in the Supersport Division, and

Sledding Superman

Legions of fans and sportswriters call twenty-three-year-old Blair Morgan "Superman." This is not only because he came out of nowhere and ended up totally dominating the 1998 Snowcross World Series (winning thirteen out of the eighteen finals of this high-profile circuit). It is also because of the way he did it—with a slew of breathtaking stunts, one of which was kicking his legs out behind him, like Superman, while riding on a sled that was moving faster than a speeding bullet.

Although Blair literally did appear on the racing circuit out of nowhere, he had been tooling around on snowmobiles since the age of four. He grew up on a farm in Prince Albert, Saskatchewan, where snowmobiling was the only way to get around. In fact, it was such a part of family life that every Sunday, the Morgan family would load up their snowmobiles—every family member had one—and go for a winter cookout.

Later, as a teen, Blair got into motocross racing. In the winter, however, he would jump back on his sled—riding it so hard that pieces would actually fall off. Because he couldn't get sledding out of his system, he decided to try snowcross racing.

In the winter of 1997, Blair entered a few small Canadian races and then decided to go all the way to the season finale in West Yellowstone, Montana. Although experts advised the unknown to race semipro, Blair—who needed the bucks to get back home to Canada—entered the pro division. He blew away his top-ranked opponents, finishing second only to snowcross legend Kirk Hibbert.

This was just the beginning. Blair went on to a string of subsequent World Series victories, including three in which top-ranked Hibbert—"The Greatest Racer Ever"—took second place to him.

His superheroic success story has turned the debonair Blair into a snowcross poster boy while making a whole new generation of teens aware of how cool snowmobiling can be. As for the Superman stunt, however, Blair doesn't recommend trying it out at home. But he brushes it off as "pretty easy": "You have such a forward motion that you just fly out behind [your machine]. Then it's like a chin-up bar, and you pull yourself back." He adds with a laugh that if you're wild enough to try it, you should "make sure you're hanging on real tight."

children, novices, women, and juniors between the ages of ten and seventeen can butt heads in various classes of the Specialty Division.

Do keep in mind that it's one thing to go smashing through the snow at record-breaking speed if you're in a race, and quite another if you're riding along a recreational trail. You don't need to go fast in order to have fun. You should always ride at a speed at which you can stop within

Trick riding is only for the experienced snowmobiler.

your line of sight. Take it slow and enjoy the scenery. Ease up on the throttle, especially when you come close to other machines, people, trees, and animals. It not only makes sense—it's the law!

Controversies

Ever since the 1960s and '70s—when snowmobiling really took off—non-snowmobilers have viewed sledders with some-what of an evil eye. This is because back in the '70s, there were few if any laws and regulations governing snowmobiling. Machines zoomed around everywhere they wanted to—in places they belonged and in places they didn't. (This was before the era of marked trails.)

Not only were the machines much more difficult to handle, but they also created an infernal ruckus—so much so that snowmobile manufacturers, clubs, race organizers, and sledders themselves decided to silence increasingly hostile critics by silencing noisy sleds. Since those days, manufacturers have drastically reduced the noise of exhaust systems, and noisy race pipes are no longer sold to trail riders. Even though these noisy race pipes are illegal, however, some riders still continue to use them. Ultimately it is up to you the sledder not to create a ruckus. Loud does not mean fast and does not mean cool; it means obnoxious. It also means closed trails.

Overall, today's snowmobilers have become much more organized, courteous, and caring. And snowmobiles themselves have become much more quiet. Nonetheless, conflicts still persist. One big problem is the conflict between snowmobilers and environmental activists. Protectors of wildlife and their natural habitats see the increased number of snowmobilers and snowmobile trails on public land as a negative thing. In some cases, they have succeeded in restricting snowmobile access to many areas. Such activists have been supported by skiers, who complain that they can't travel through the wilderness anymore without running into snowmobile tracks.

At the same time, some private landowners (in states such as Vermont and Maine, 90 percent of snowmobiling trails cut through private property) are also complaining

Popular areas can become quite crowded.

about crowded trails and the noise created by both humans and their machines. Even though they have always been very cooperative in designing trails with local snow-mobiling clubs, some of these owners are now closing their gates to snowmobiles.

Because of these very real complaints, snowmobiling clubs have been getting organized and getting involved. Along with forestry services and private landowners, club members plan trails that respect both the environment and other outdoor recreationists. They have become involved in creating and safeguarding laws concerning snowmobile trails and safety. In a big way, they have attempted to show that snowmobilers can be good neighbors who can have a positive effect on a snowbelt community. In the end, this is the only manner in which snowmobiling as a sport, an activity, and a wintry way of life can continue to grow.

6 Sled Heads

It was one of those truly spectacular winter sunrises. Actually, it was still mostly dark, but Sam couldn't wait to get out on the trail and feel the soft white powder flying through the air around him as he zoomed through the forests.

"Hey, you guys! Wake up!" Sam yelled, walking into his parents' room and turning the light on and off repeatedly.

Sam's father rolled over and groaned. "Sam, are you nuts?"

Sam's mother sat up and yawned. "What time is it, honey?"

"Time to hit the trail, Mom! Come on, you two! Shake a leg!"

Sam's father turned to his wife and moaned, "Why, oh, why did I turn this kid on to snowmobiling? Life will never again be the same."

"Come on, honey," said Sam's mother, climbing out from under the covers. "We're sled heads now. Got to hit the powder."

While Sam's parents got showered and dressed, Sam woke up his younger sister, Patty Sue, and then went into the kitchen to rustle up a hearty breakfast of scrambled eggs. Outside the windows of their rented vacation cabin, a pink sun was spreading its light across the breathtaking winter landscape of Michigan's Upper Peninsula.

A spectacular day for a ride!

This snowmobiling vacation—the family's first—had been the best time Sam had ever had. Since today was their last full day of sledding before heading home to Vermont, Sam wanted to take advantage of every minute. Even though it was already the end of March, hopefully there would still be enough snow left in Vermont for at least a couple more weekends of sledding. Too bad that April was just around the corner, and soon spring would be rearing its ugly head.

The thought of winter ending made Sam sad. Ever since he had learned how to snowmobile, this winter had been the best ever. He had joined his local snowmobiling club, and he and his dad had gone on some great outings with the other members. When father and son returned home at night, tired but elated after a long day in the saddle, they couldn't stop talking about sledding—about the animals they saw, the trails they had navigated, the new riding techniques they had learned. Their endless snowmobile babble made both Sam's mom and Patty Sue so jealous that they had decided to take up snowmobiling as well. Now the whole family was addicted, and their garage was stuffed with snowmobiles and snowmobile equipment.

Sam sighed as he cracked open the eggs and stirred them around in the frying pan. He would really miss sledding for the next six months. However, he was looking forward to volunteering his time to help groom trails with other members of his snowmobiling club. He was also going to take a more advanced safety and certification course that would allow him to teach snowmobiling techniques to younger kids. And the club itself had all sorts of cool activities planned to raise money for trail maintenance—a spring fair, a summer hike-a-thon, and an auction of snow-mobile helmets painted by local artists. Sam, along with a couple of his new sledding buddies, Mira and Wallace, were on the organizing committee.

He snapped out of his daydreaming as he felt his mother mussing his hair.

"Yo! Sled head!" she said, laughing. "Serve up those eggs! We've got a whole lot of snow to ride through today!"

Glossary

Avalanche
A sudden, dangerous rush of snow and ice descending a mountainside.

Fiberglass
A material made from a mixture of plastic and glass.

Groomed trail
A trail that is specially designed, cleared, and marked for riding.

Hypothermia
A life-threatening condition in which your body temperature plunges.

Insulator
A material or substance that blocks heat from escaping.

Integrated trails
Individual trails that are connected to one another.

Polycarbonate
A type of tough, transparent plastic.

Powder hound
Slang for a person who loves to ride snowmobiles.

Shock absorber
Device used to absorb sudden shocks.

Sled

Slang for snowmobile.

Sled head

Slang for snowmobile freak.

Snowcross racing

Professional snowmobile racing across snowy terrain.

Snow plan

Your planned route and destination along with a description of
your machine.

Suspension system

Springs supporting the upper part of a motor vehicle.

Track system

System of two endless metal belts that allows a vehicle to travel.

Visor

The overhanging front piece of a helmet that acts as an eye shield.

Resources

Organizations

The American Council of Snowmobile Associations
271 Woodland Pass, Suite 216
East Lansing, MI 48823
(517) 351-4362

Blue Ribbon Coalition
P.O. Box 5449
Pocatello, ID 83202
(208) 237-1557
Web site: http://www.sharetrails.org/

Canadian Council of Snowmobile Organizations
106 Saunders Road, Unit 12
Barrie, ON L4M 6E7
(705) 725-1121
Web site: http://www.ccso-ccom.ca/

International Snowmobile Manufacturers Association (ISMA)
1640 Haslett Road, Suite 170
Haslett, MI 48840
(517) 339-7788

International Snowmobiling Hall of Fame
25929 County Road 59
Bovey, MN 55709
(218) 245-1725
Web site: http://www.snowmobile.org/

Tread Lightly! Inc.
298 24th Street, Suite 325
Ogden, UT 84401
(800) 966-9900
Web site: http://www.treadlightly.org/index.html

Web Sites

American Snowcross Racing Association
http://www.snowcross.com/asra.html

American Snowmobiler
http://www.amsnow.com/

Canadian Snowcross Racing Association
http://www.snowcross.com/csra.html

ESPN Extreme Games
http://espn.go.com/extreme/xgames/

Kid's Club—Snowmobile Discovery Book
http://198.59.8.50/trails/snowmobile/kids/index.html

SnowConnection Magazine
http://www.snowconnection.com/

Snowmobiling Online
http://www.off-road.com/snowmobile/index.html

Snow Tracks—Snowmobiling Trail Conditions Throughout the United States
    and Canada
http://www.snowtracks.com/

For Further Reading

Magazines

American Snowmobile Magazine
SnoWest Magazine
Snow Goer
SnowRider Magazine
Snow Week

Videos

Safe Riders: You Make Snowmobiling Safe

Books

Armentrout, David, and Patricia Armentrout. *Extreme Machines on Ice and Snow.*
Vero Beach, FL: Rourke Press, 1998.

Conover, Garrett, and Alexandra Conover. *A Snow Walker's Companion: Winter Trail Skills from the Far North.* New York: McGraw-Hill, 1994.

Gorman, Stephen. *AMC Guide to Winter Camping: Wilderness Travel and Adventure in the Cold-Weather Months.* Boston, MA: Appalachian Mountain Club Books, 1991.

Hallam, David, and James Hallam. *Snowmobiling: The Sledder's Complete Handbook.* Denver, CO: Fun on Snow Publications, 1999.

Ilg, Steve, and Gary Johnson. *Outdoor Performance.* Boulder, CO: Johnson Books, 1999.

Kreissman, Bern. *The Complete Winter Sports Safety Manual: Staying Safe & Warm Snowshoeing, Skiing, Snowboarding, Snowmobiling, and Camping.* Helena, MT: Falcon Press Publishing Co., 1997.

McClung, David, and Peter Schaerer. *Avalanche Handbook*. Seattle, WA: The Mountaineers Books, 1993.

Stark, Peter, and Steven M. Krauzer. *Winter Adventure: A Complete Guide to Winter Sports*. New York: W. W. Norton, 1996.

Weiss, Hal. *Secrets of Warmth: For Comfort or Survival*. Seattle, WA: The Mountaineers Books, 1999.

Index

Credits

About the Author
Michael Sommers is the author of many books for young readers and is an aspiring powder hound.

Photo Credits
Cover photo © Polaris Snowmobiles. p. 5 © FPG International/Gary Buss; pp. 7, 22, 32, 54 © Mountain Stock/Hank deVre; pp. 9, 51 © Corbis/Richard Hamilton Smith; pp. 14, 16, 18 © Carl Eliason & Company, Inc.; p. 19 © Corbis/Bettman; p. 20 © Tim Bottomley/Mountain Stock; pp. 25, 28 © ALLSPORT/Mike Powell; p. 26 © Polaris Snowmobiles; p. 31 courtesy of International Snowmobile Manufacturer's Association (ISMA); p. 39 © Kevin Woodward/Mountain Stock; p. 41 © Corbis/O. Alamany & E. Vicens; p. 42 © ALLSPORT/ Didier Givois; pp. 45, 49 © ALLSPORT/Jamie Squire; p. 47 © Wayne Davis Photography.

Series Design and Layout
Oliver H. Rosenberg